W9-AMY-170

The Sound of Music
SOUVENIR FOLIO

Music by
RICHARD RODGERS

Lyrics by
OSCAR HAMMERSTEIN II

Additional Words & Music
for the film version by
RICHARD RODGERS

Book by
HOWARD LINDSAY and RUSSELL CROUSE

Screenplay by
ERNEST LEHMAN

Suggested by "The Trapp Family Singers" by
MARIA AUGUSTA TRAPP

THE SOUND OF MUSIC Souvenir Folio contains all the pertinent information and songs from the original musical play and the musical film. A sequence of photographs from both versions provides an illuminating panorama of this great family entertainment. Photos from the film courtesy of 20th Century-Fox Film Corporation. Photos from the original stage production courtesy of Richard Halliday, Leland Heyward, and Rodgers & Hammerstein.

WILLIAMSON MUSIC™
A RODGERS AND HAMMERSTEIN COMPANY

Exclusively Distributed by
Hal Leonard Publishing Corporation
7777 West Bluemound Road P.O. Box 13819 Milwaukee, WI 53213

Applications for performance of this work, whether legitimate, stock, amateur, or foreign, should be addressed to:
RODGERS & HAMMERSTEIN LIBRARY
598 Madison Avenue
New York, NY 10022

The Sound of Music

Produced by LELAND HAYWARD, RICHARD HALLIDAY,
RICHARD RODGERS and OSCAR HAMMERSTEIN II
November 16, 1959 at the Lunt-Fontanne Theatre, New York City

Directed by
VINCENT J. DONEHUE

Musical Numbers Staged by JOE LAYTON
Scenic Production by OLIVER SMITH
Costumes by LUCINDA BALLARD
Mary Martin's clothes by MAINBOCHER
Lighting by JEAN ROSENTHAL
Orchestrations by ROBERT RUSSELL BENNETT
Choral Arrangements by TRUDE RITTMAN
Musical Direction by FREDERICK DVONCH

Cast of Characters
(*In order of appearance*)

MARIA RAINER, *a postulant at Nonnberg Abbey*	Mary Martin
SISTER BERTHE, *mistress of novices*	Elizabeth Howell
SISTER MARGARETTA, *mistress of postulants*	Muriel O'Malley
THE MOTHER ABBESS	Patricia Neway
SISTER SOPHIA	Karen Shepard
CAPTAIN GEORG VON TRAPP	Theodore Bikel
FRANZ, *the butler*	John Randolph
FRAU SCHMIDT, *the housekeeper*	Nan McFarland
LIESL	Lauri Peters
FRIEDRICH	William Snowden
LOUISA	Kathy Dunn
KURT *children of Captain Von Trapp*	Joseph Stewart
BRIGITTA	Marilyn Rogers
MARTA	Marilyn Susan Locke
GRETL	Evanna Lien
ROLF GRUBER	Brian Davies
ELSA SCHRAEDER	Marion Marlowe
URSULA	Luce Ennis
MAX DETWEILER	Kurt Kasznar
HERR ZELLER	Stefan Gierasch
BARON ELBERFELD	Kirby Smith
A POSTULANT	Sue Yaeger
ADMIRAL VON SCHREIBER	Michael Gorrin

NEIGHBORS *of Captain Von Trapp*, NUNS, NOVICES, POSTULATES,
CONTESTANTS *in the Festival Concert:* Joanne Birks, Patricia Brooks,
June Card, Dorothy Dallas, Ceil Delly, Luce Ennis, Cleo Fry, Barbara
George, Joey Heatherton, Lucas Hoving, Patricia Kelly, Maria Kova,
Shirley Mendonca, Kathy Miller, Lorna Nash, Keith Prentice, Nancy
Reeves, Bernice Saunders, Connie Sharman, Gloria Stevens, Tatiana
Troyanos, Mimi Vondra.

THE SOUND OF MUSIC

A 20th CENTURY-FOX Motion Picture Presentation
World premiere March 2, 1965 at the Rivoli Theatre, New York

Produced and Directed by
ROBERT WISE

Associate Producer SAUL CHAPLIN
Music Supervised, Arranged and Conducted by IRWIN KOSTAL
Production Designed by BORIS LEVEN
Director of Photography TED McCORD, A.S.C.
Choreography by MARC BREAUX *and* DEE DEE WOOD
Costumes by DOROTHY JEAKINS

Cast of Characters

MARIA RAINER	. . . .	Julie Andrews
CAPTAIN GEORG VON TRAPP	. . . .	Christopher Plummer
ELSA SCHRAEDER, *the baroness*	. . . .	Eleanor Parker
MAX DETWEILER	. . . .	Richard Haydn
THE MOTHER ABBESS	. . . .	Peggy Wood
LIESL		Charmian Carr
LOUISA		Heather Menzies
FRIEDRICH		Nicolas Hammond
KURT	*children of Captain von Trapp* . .	Duane Chase
BRIGITTA		Angela Cartwright
MARTA		Debbie Turner
GRETL		Kym Karath
SISTER MARGARETTA	. . . .	Anna Lee
SISTER BERTHE	. . . .	Portia Nelson
HERR ZELLER	. . . .	Ben Wright
ROLF GRUBER	. . . .	Daniel Truhitte
FRAU SCHMIDT	. . . .	Norma Varden
FRANZ	. . . .	Gil Stuart
SISTER SOPHIA	. . . .	Marni Nixon
SISTER BERNICE	. . . .	Evadne Baker
BARONESS EBBERFELD	. . . .	Doris Lloyd

The Bil Baird Marionettes

Second Unit Supervision MAURICE ZUBERANO
Vocal Supervision ROBERT RUCKER
Film Editor WILLIAM REYNOLDS, A.C.E.
Additional Photography PAUL BEESON, B.S.C.
Sound by MURRAY SPIVACK *and* BERNARD FREERICKS
Unit Production Manager SAUL WURTZEL
Assistant Director RIDGEWAY CALLOW
Dialogue Coach PAMELA DANOVA
Music Editor ROBERT MAYER
Set Decorations WALTER M. SCOTT *and* RUBY LEVITT
Special Photographic Effects L. B. ABBOTT, A.S.C., *and* EMIL KOSA, Jr.
Sound Recording Supervised by FRED HYNES *and* JAMES CORCORAN
Makeup by BEN NYE
Hair Styles by MARGARET DONOVAL
Aerial views photographed with MCS-70 Camera
Color by DELUXE

The Story

The Austrian Alps, alive with the sound of music, have a special appeal for Maria, a postulant at the Salzburg Abbey. Her frequent absences, however, are a source of discord at the Abbey and give rise to doubts as to her qualifications. Hence the Mother Abbess sends Maria to serve as governess for the widowed Captain von Trapp, who runs his home with naval precision.

His seven children are slow in warming up to Maria but when the Captain goes to Vienna she wins them over with understanding and humor, while teaching them to sing. Returning from Vienna Capt. von Trapp is upset by his children's lack of discipline but is soon so touched by their singing he joins in.

Before long Maria realizes she is in love with the Captain and, horrified, returns to the Abbey. The Mother Abbess convinces her that love is also a holy thing and with the children's blessing Maria and the Captain are married. During the honeymoon Austria is annexed to Hitler's Germany, making a difficult situation for the Captain who has been ordered to return to the navy. Entering the Salzburg Festival provides a way out and with the aid of the nuns they escape to the hills and freedom.

Musical Contents

The Sound Of Music

Words by
OSCAR HAMMERSTEIN II

Music by
RICHARD RODGERS

Molto moderato (tenderly)

My day in the hills has come to an end, I know. A star has come out to tell me it's time to go. But deep in the dark green shad-ows are voic-es that urge me to stay. So I pause and I wait and I lis-ten for one more sound, For

1077-5

Copyright © 1959 by Richard Rodgers and Oscar Hammerstein II
Copyright Renewed
WILLIAMSON MUSIC owner of publication and allied rights throughout the world.
International Copyright Secured   All Rights Reserved

6

one more love-ly thing that the hills might say.

Refrain *(moderately, with warm expression)*

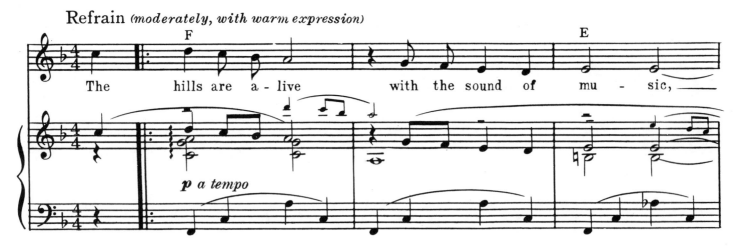

The hills are a-live with the sound of mu - sic,

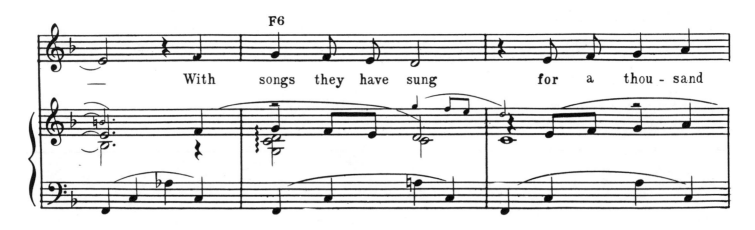

With songs they have sung for a thou-sand

years. The hills fill my heart with the sound of

1077 - 5

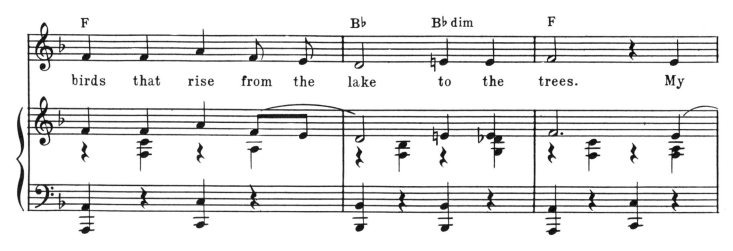

1077-5

8

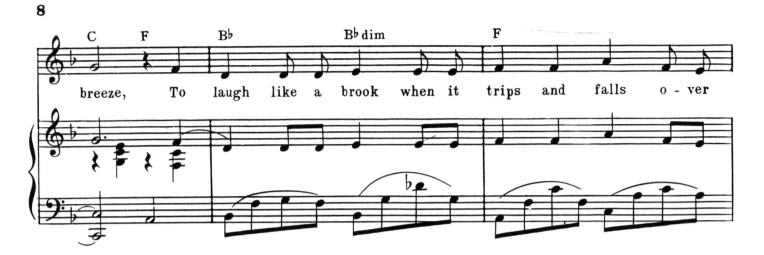

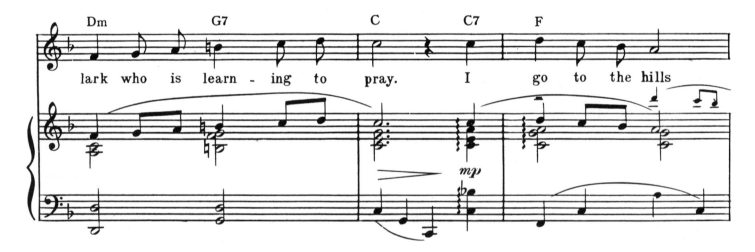

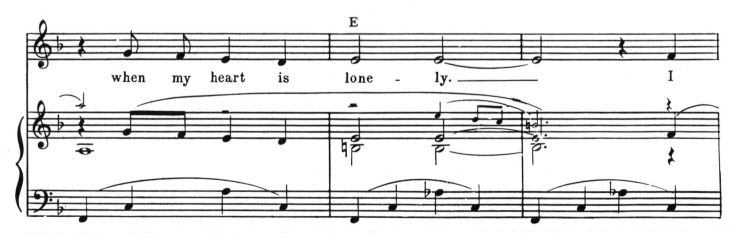

1077-5

know I will hear what I've heard be - fore.

My heart will be blessed with the sound of

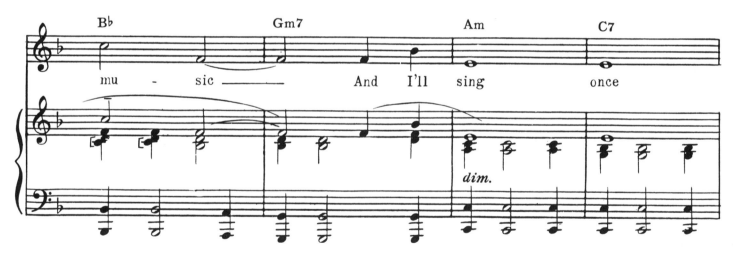

mu - sic And I'll sing once

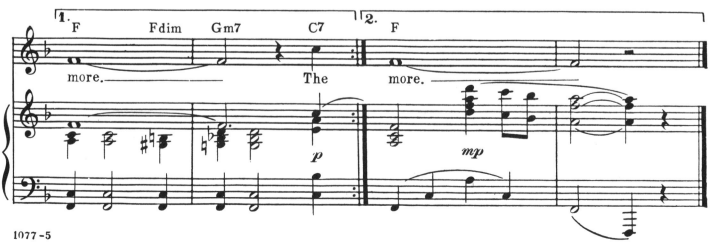

more. The more.

1077-5

"The Sound Of Music"

Maria

Words by
OSCAR HAMMERSTEIN II

Music by
RICHARD RODGERS

Copyright © 1959 by Richard Rodgers and Oscar Hammerstein II
Copyright Renewed
WILLIAMSON MUSIC owner of publication and allied rights throughout the world.
International Copyright Secured   All Rights Reserved

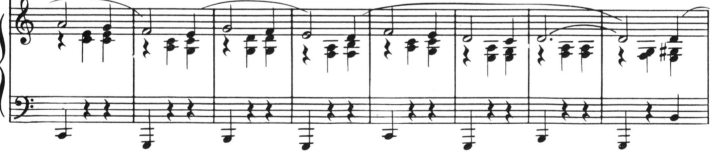

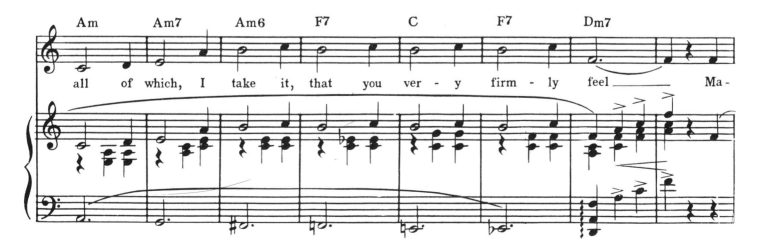

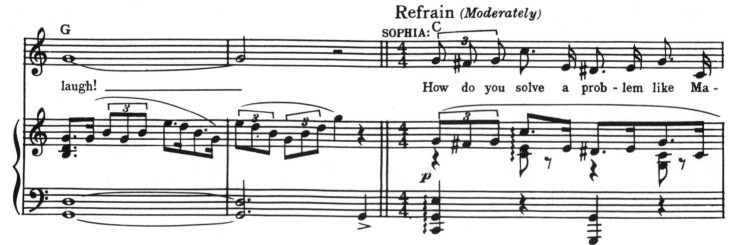

1074-9

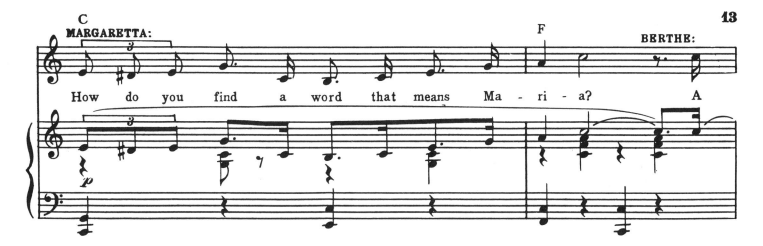

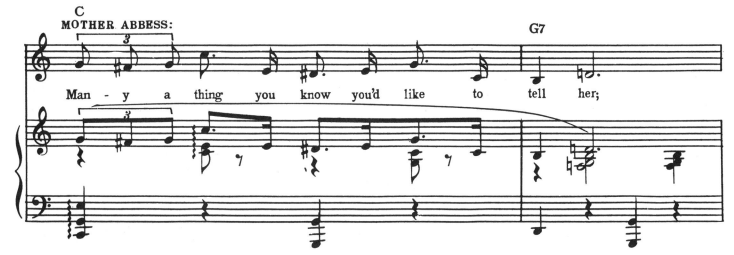

how do you make her stay and lis-ten to all you say?

MOTHER ABBESS:
How do you keep a wave up-on the sand?

MARGARETTA:
Oh,

how do you solve a prob-lem like Ma-ri-a?

MOTHER ABBESS:
How do you hold a

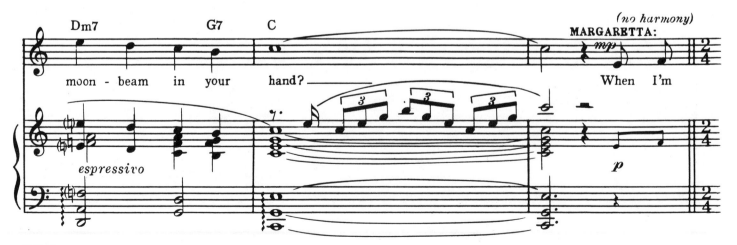

moon-beam in your hand? _____

MARGARETTA:
When I'm

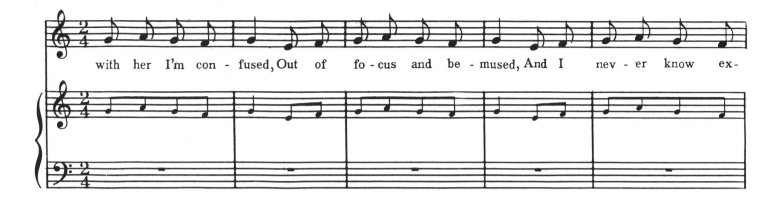

with her I'm con - fused, Out of fo - cus and be - mused, And I nev - er know ex-

act - ly where I am._____ **SOPHIA:** Un - pre - dict - a - ble as weath - er, She's as

flight - y as a feath - er, **MARGARETTA:** She's a dar - ling, **BERTHE:** She's a de - mon, **MARGARETTA:** She's a lamb.____

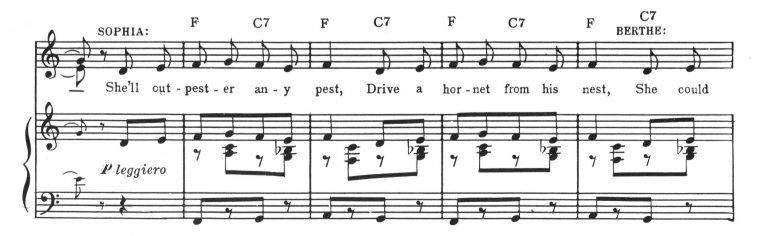

SOPHIA: She'll out - pest - er an - y pest, Drive a hor - net from his nest, She could

1074-9

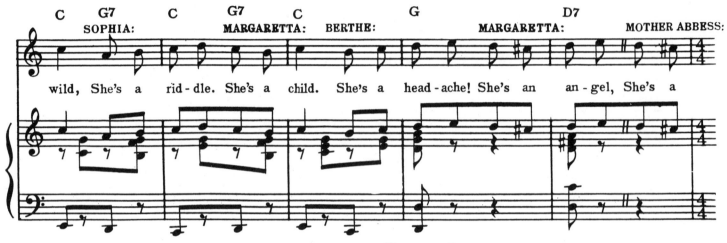

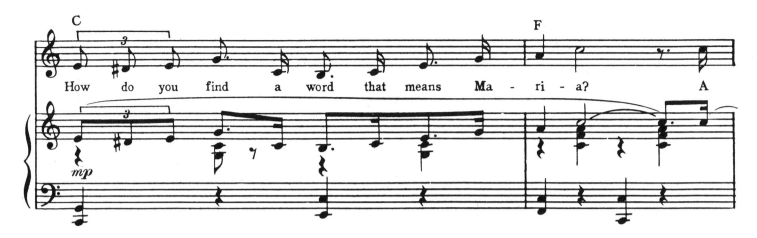

how do you make her stay and lis-ten to all you say?

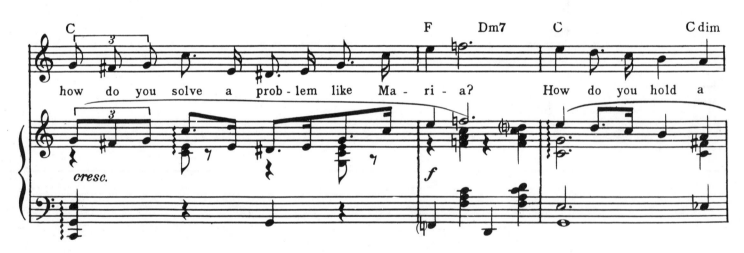

How do you keep a wave up-on the sand? Oh,

how do you solve a prob-lem like Ma-ri-a? How do you hold a

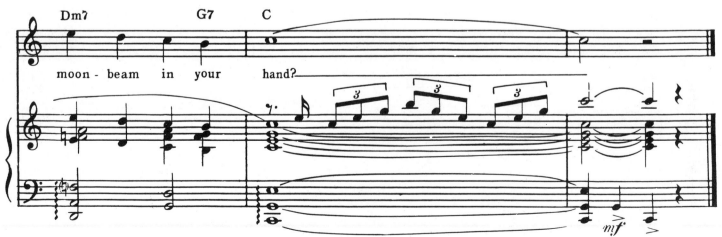

moon-beam in your hand?

Photos courtesy 20th Century-Fox Film Corporation

I Have Confidence

Words and Music by
RICHARD RODGERS

Allegretto

Refrain

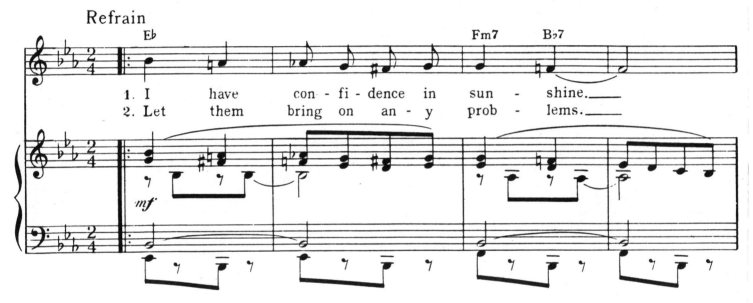

1. I have con-fi-dence in sun-shine._____
2. Let them bring on an-y prob-lems._____

I have con-fi-dence in rain._____
I'll do bet-ter than my best._____

1227-4

Copyright © 1964 by Richard Rodgers
WILLIAMSON MUSIC owner of publication and allied rights throughout the world.
International Copyright Secured   All Rights Reserved

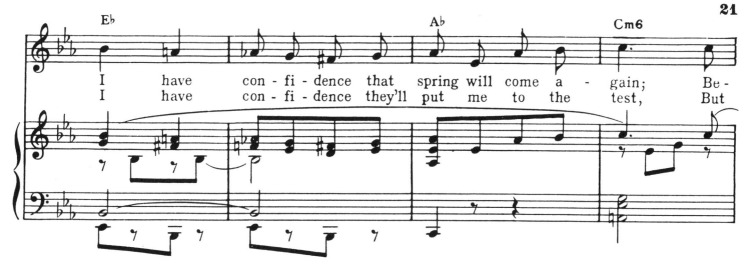

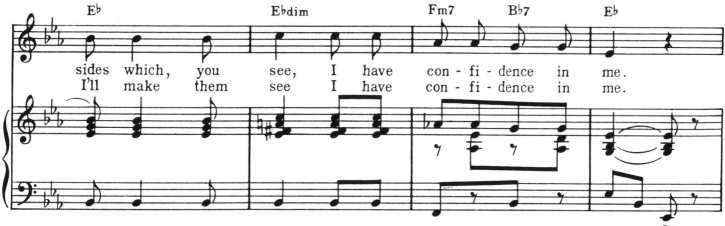

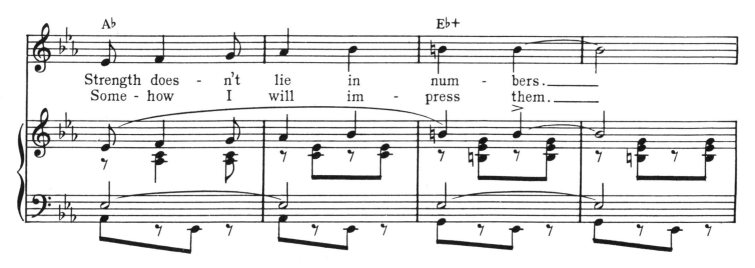

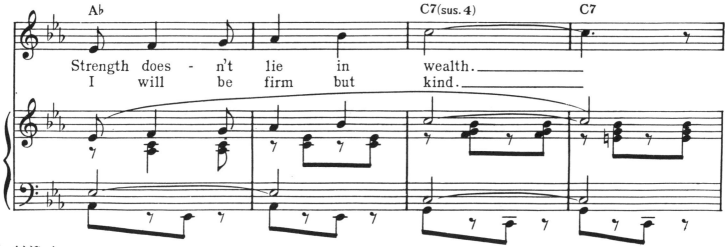

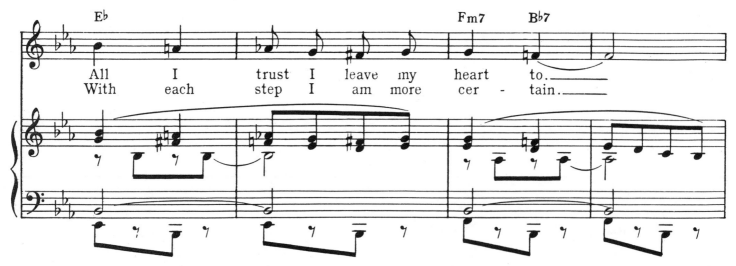

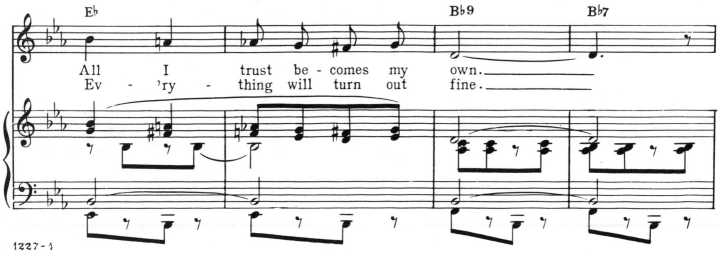

I have con-fi-dence in con-fi-dence a-lone; Be-
I have con-fi-dence the world can all be mine. They'll

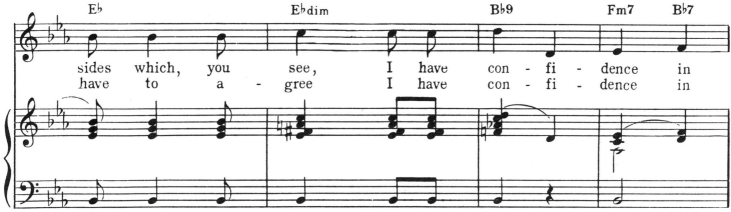

sides which, you see, I have con-fi-dence in
have to a-gree I have con-fi-dence in

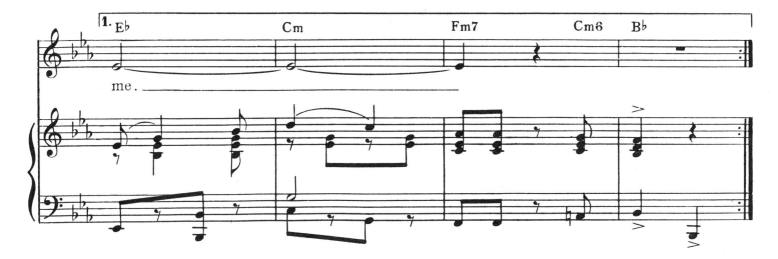

1. me.

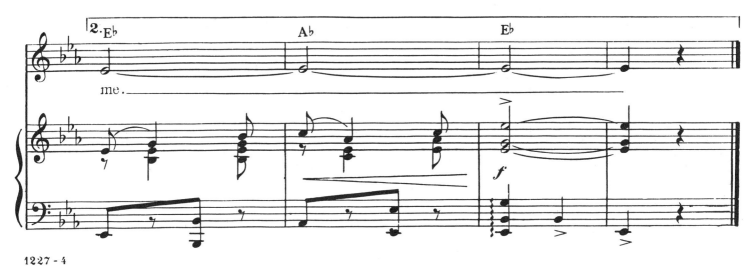

2. me.

"The Sound Of Music"

My Favorite Things

Words by
OSCAR HAMMERSTEIN II

Music by
RICHARD RODGERS

Rain - drops on ros - es and whisk - ers on kit - tens, Bright cop - per

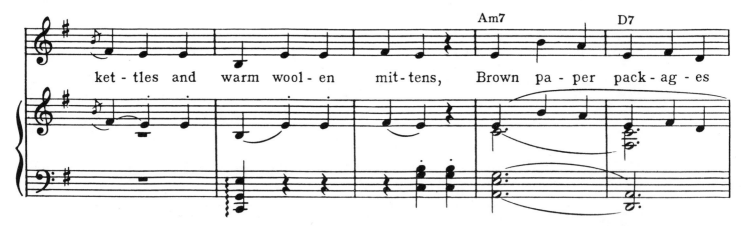

ket - tles and warm wool - en mit - tens, Brown pa - per pack - ag - es

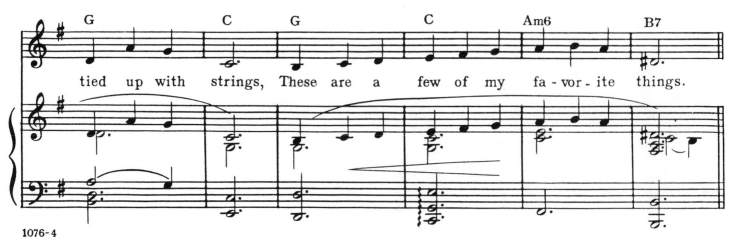

tied up with strings, These are a few of my fa - vor - ite things.

1076-4

Copyright © 1959 by Richard Rodgers and Oscar Hammerstein II
Copyright Renewed
WILLIAMSON MUSIC owner of publication and allied rights throughout the world.
International Copyright Secured   All Rights Reserved

Girls in white dress - es with blue sat - in sash - es, Snow-flakes that
stay on my nose and eye - lash - es, Sil - ver white win - ters that

melt in - to springs, These are a few of my fa - vor - ite things.

When the dog bites, When the bee stings,

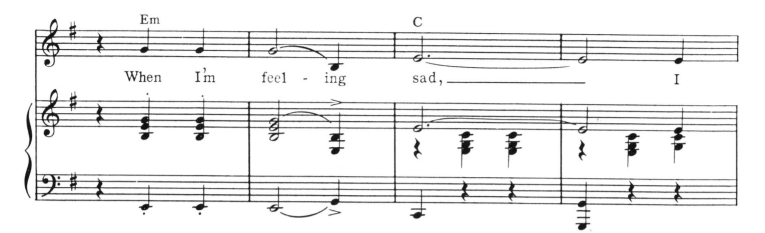

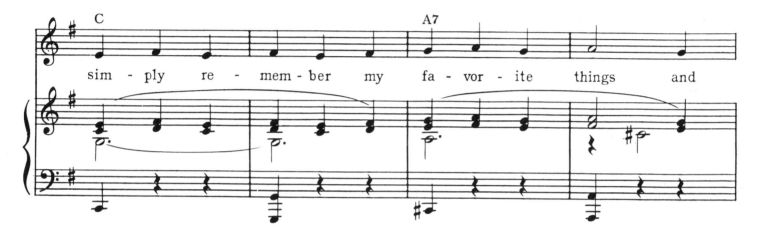

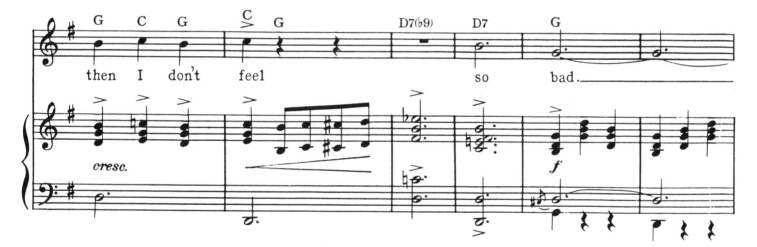

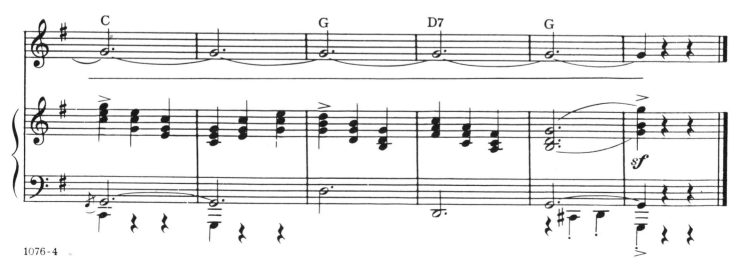

1076-4

"The Sound Of Music"

Do-Re-Mi

Words by
OSCAR HAMMERSTEIN II

Music by
RICHARD RODGERS

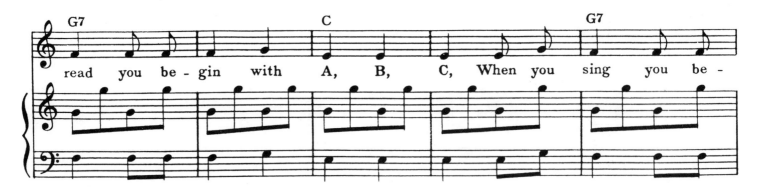

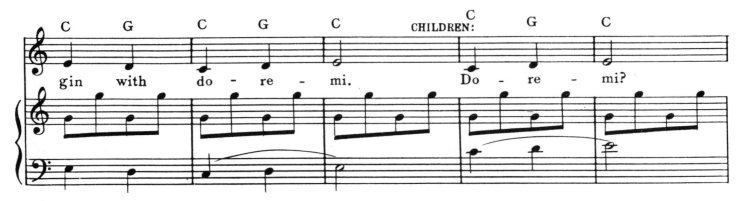

Copyright © 1959 by Richard Rodgers and Oscar Hammerstein II
Copyright Renewed
WILLIAMSON MUSIC owner of publication and allied rights throughout the world.
International Copyright Secured   All Rights Reserved

Refrain *(in spirited tempo)*

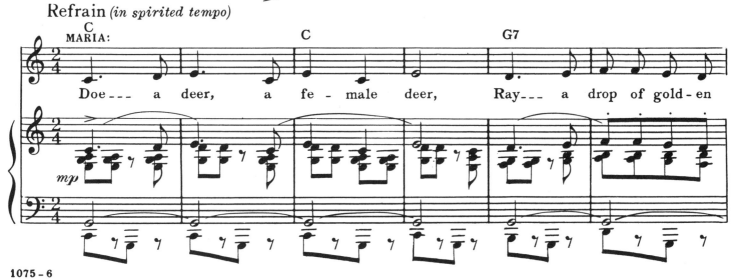

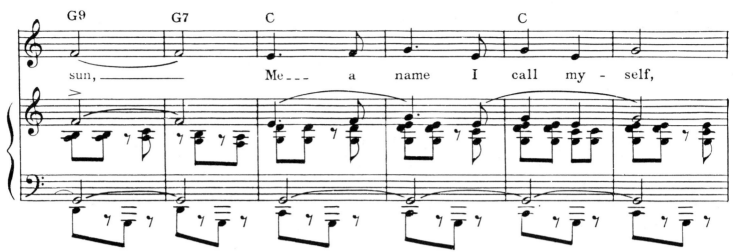

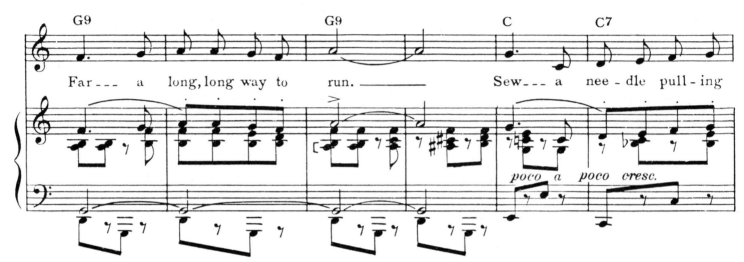

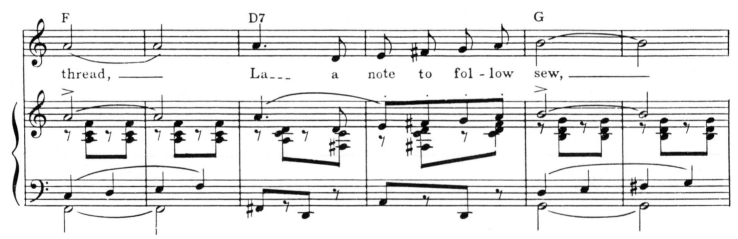

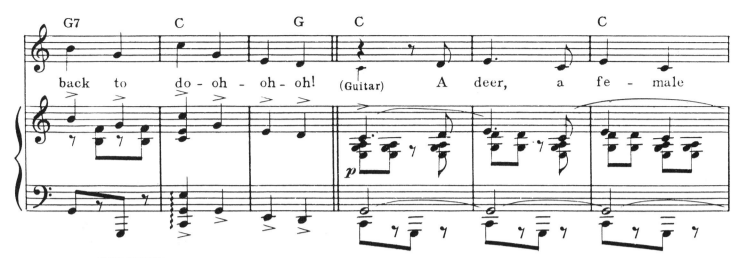

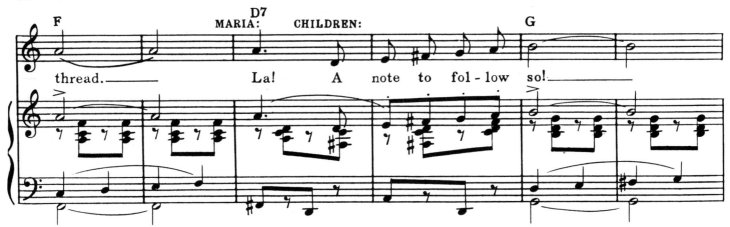

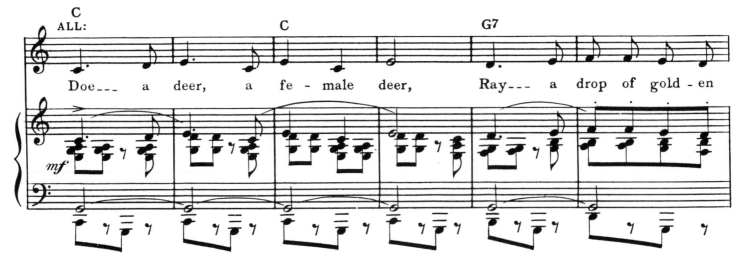

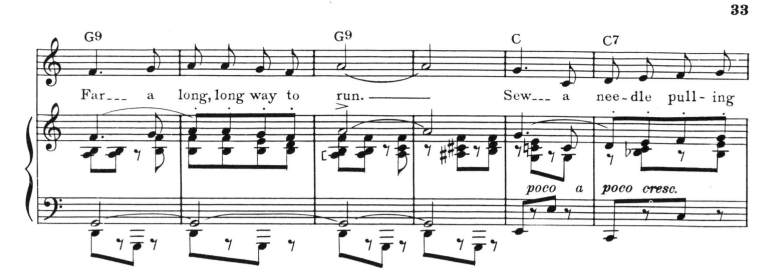

Something Good

Words and Music by
RICHARD RODGERS

1208-3

Copyright © 1964 by Richard Rodgers
WILLIAMSON MUSIC owner of publication and allied rights throughout the world.
International Copyright Secured   All Rights Reserved

must have been a mo-ment of truth._____ For here you are, Stand-ing there, Lov-ing me,_____ Wheth-er or not you should._____ So, some-where in my youth or child-hood_____ I must have done

36

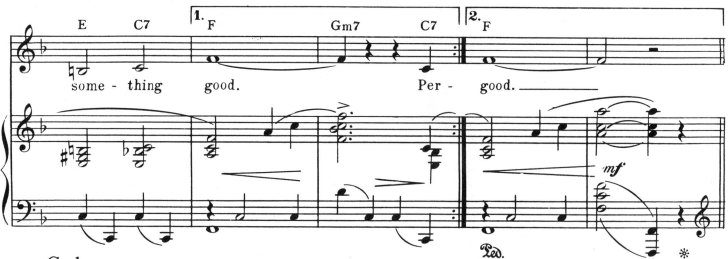

some - thing good.　Per - good.

Coda

Noth-ing comes from noth-ing,　Noth-ing ev - er could.　So,

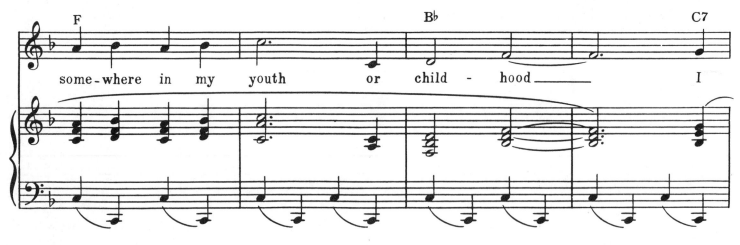

some-where in my youth　or child - hood　I

must have done　some - thing good.

1208-3

Photos by Friedman-Abeles

Photo by Toni Frissell

Sixteen Going On Seventeen

Words by
OSCAR HAMMERSTEIN II

Music by
RICHARD RODGERS

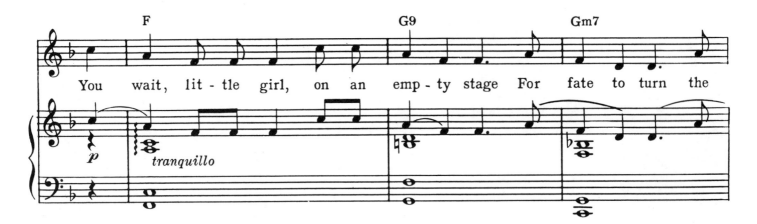

You wait, lit-tle girl, on an emp-ty stage For fate to turn the

light on. Your life, lit-tle girl, is an emp-ty page That

men will want to write on, to write on. ___

1073-8

Copyright © 1959 by Richard Rodgers and Oscar Hammerstein II
Copyright Renewed
WILLIAMSON MUSIC owner of publication and allied rights throughout the world.
International Copyright Secured   All Rights Reserved

Refrain (*Assai moderato*)

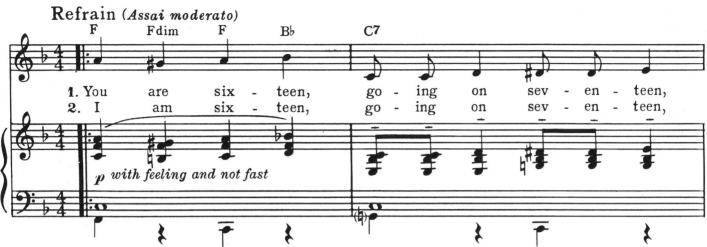

1. You are six-teen, go-ing on sev-en-teen,
2. I am six-teen, go-ing on sev-en-teen,

p with feeling and not fast

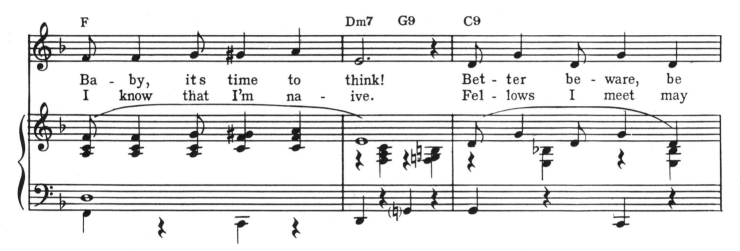

Ba-by, its time to think! Bet-ter be-ware, be
I know that I'm na-ive. Fel-lows I meet may

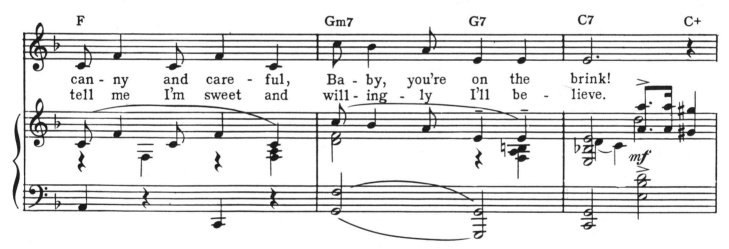

can-ny and care-ful, Ba-by, you're on the brink!
tell me I'm sweet and will-ing-ly I'll be-lieve.

mf

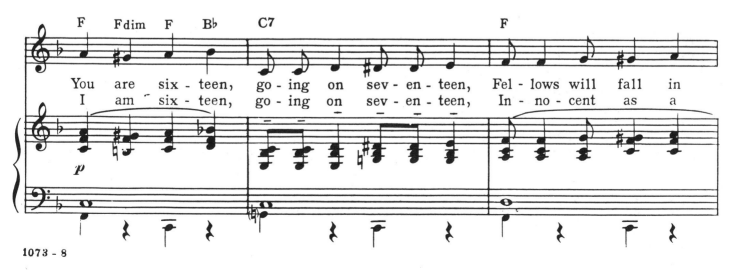

You are six-teen, go-ing on sev-en-teen, Fel-lows will fall in
I am six-teen, go-ing on sev-en-teen, In-no-cent as a

p

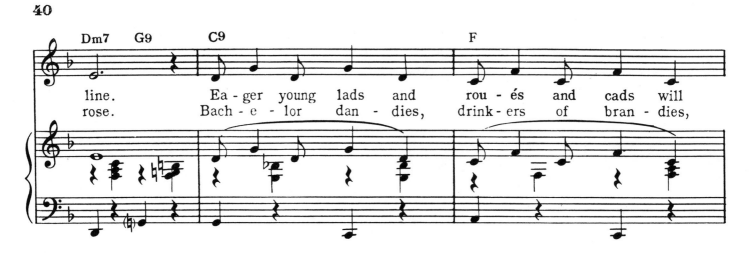

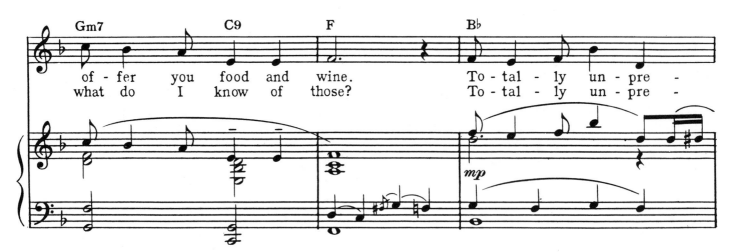

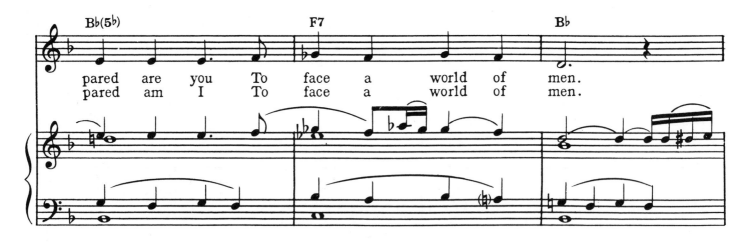

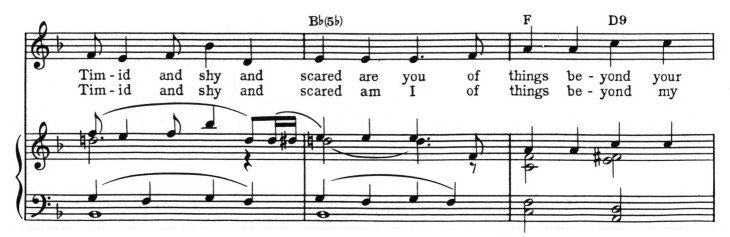

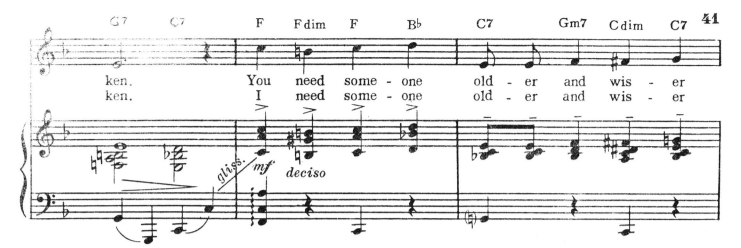

ken.   You need some - one old - er and wis - er
ken.   I need some - one old - er and wis - er

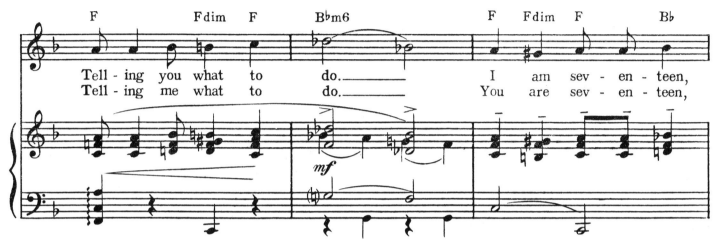

Tell - ing you what to do._____ I am sev - en - teen,
Tell - ing me what to do._____ You are sev - en - teen,

go - ing on eight - een, I'll___ take care___ of you.
go - ing on eight - een, I'll___ de - pend___ on

you._____ you.

42

Interlude

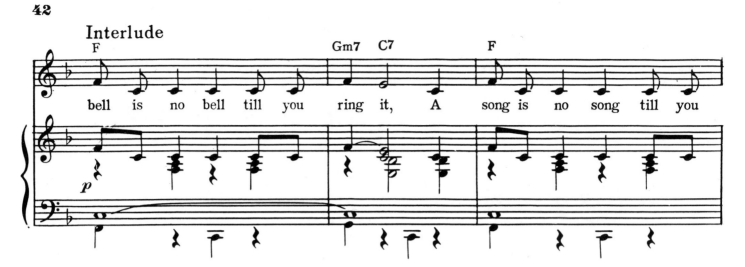

bell is no bell till you ring it, A song is no song till you

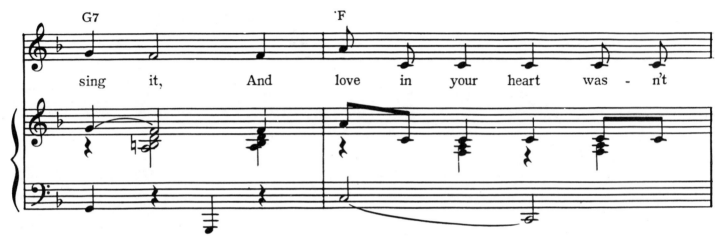

sing it, And love in your heart was - n't

put there to stay, Love is - n't love till you

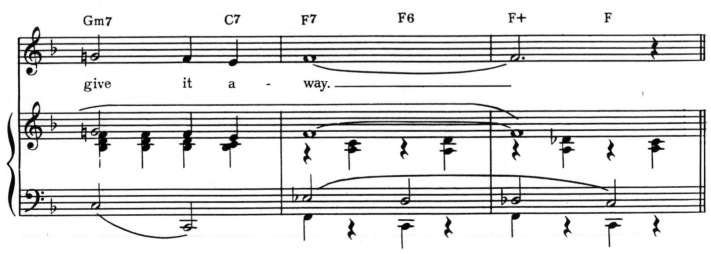

give it a - way.

1073- 8

3rd Refrain *(Assai moderato)*

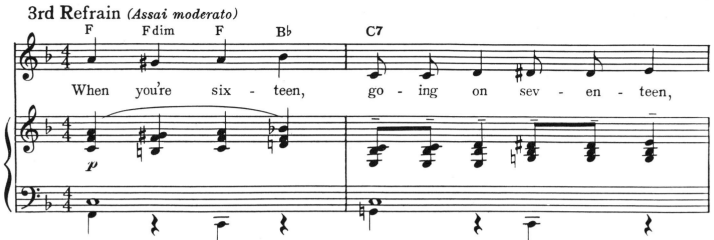

When you're six - teen, go - ing on sev - en - teen,

Wait - ing for life to start, Some - bod - y kind who

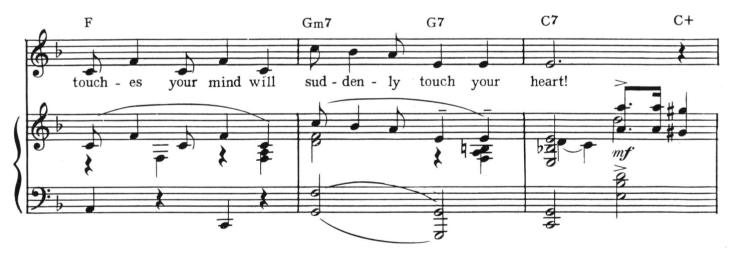

touch - es your mind will sud - den - ly touch your heart!

When that hap - pens, af - ter it hap - pens, noth - ing is quite the

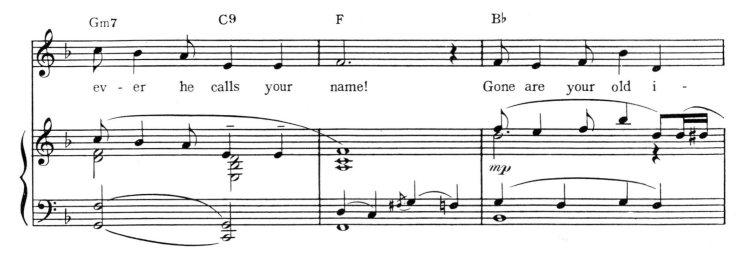

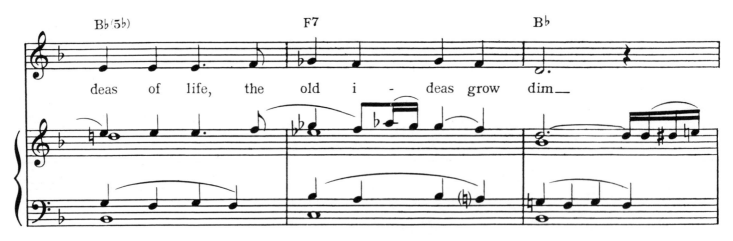

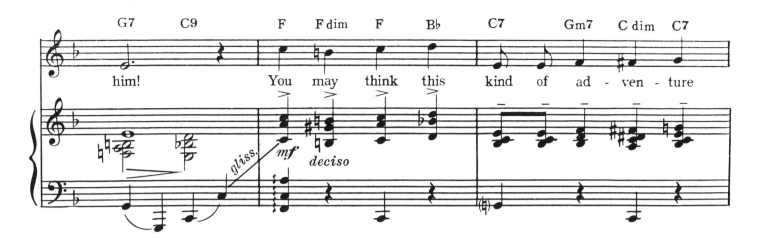

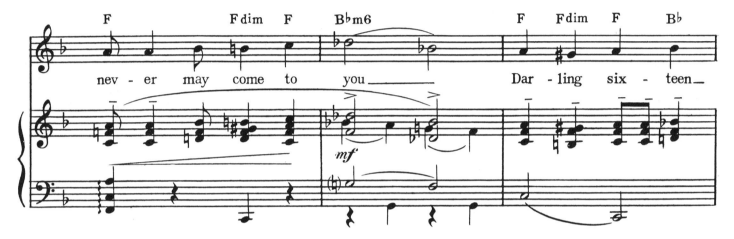

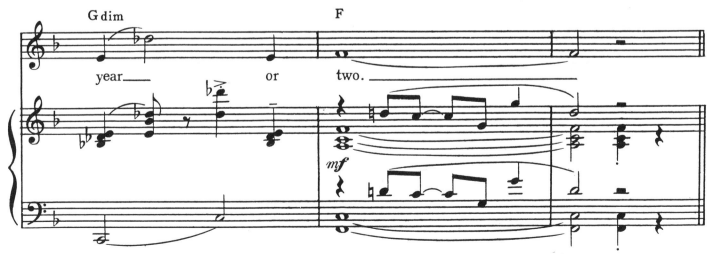

"The Sound Of Music"

The Lonely Goatherd

Words by
OSCAR HAMMERSTEIN II

Music by
RICHARD RODGERS

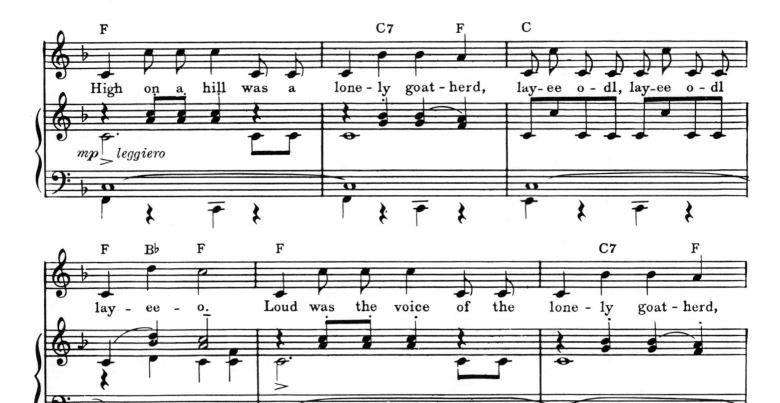

Copyright © 1959 by Richard Rodgers and Oscar Hammerstein II
Copyright Renewed
WILLIAMSON MUSIC owner of publication and allied rights throughout the world.
International Copyright Secured   All Rights Reserved

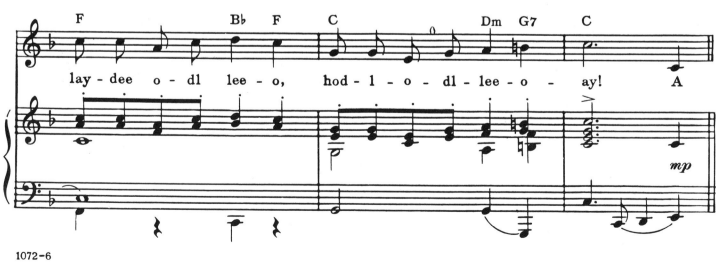

prince on the bridge of a cas-tle moat, heard: lay-ee o-dl, lay-ee o-dl lay-ee — o.

Men on a road, with a load to tote, heard: lay-ee o-dl, lay-ee o-dl - o.

Men, in the midst of a ta-ble d'hote, heard: lay-ee o-dl, lay-ee o-dl lay-ee - o.

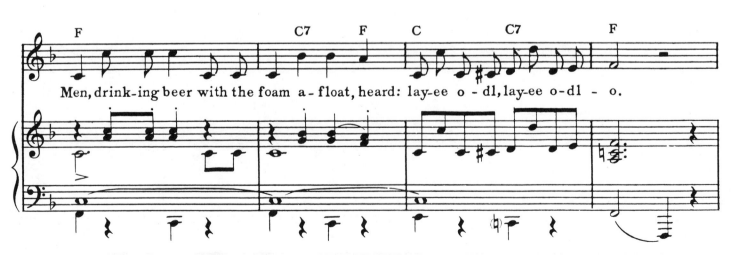

Men, drink-ing beer with the foam a-float, heard: lay-ee o-dl, lay-ee o-dl - o.

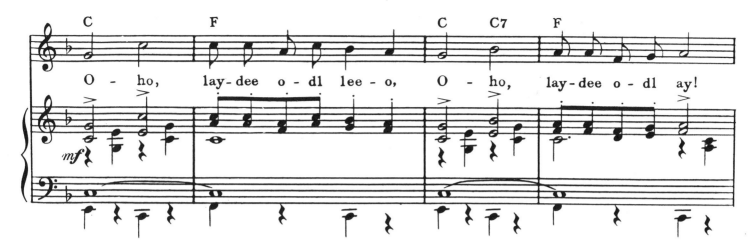

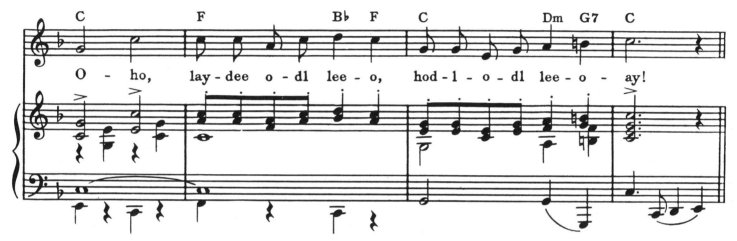

1072-6

Soon her ma-ma, with a gleam-ing gloat, heard: lay-ee o-dl, lay-ee o-dl lay-ee-o.

What a du-et for a girl and goat-herd: lay-ee o-dl, lay-ee o-dl - o.

O - ho, lay-dee o-dl lee o, O - ho, lay-dee o-dl ay!

O - ho, lay-dee o-dl lee-o, hod-l-o-dl lee-o - ay!

Coda

So Long, Farewell

Words by
OSCAR HAMMERSTEIN II

Music by
RICHARD RODGERS

Copyright © 1959, 1960 by Richard Rodgers and Oscar Hammerstein II
Copyright Renewed
WILLIAMSON MUSIC owner of publication and allied rights throughout the world.
International Copyright Secured   All Rights Reserved

hate to go and leave this pret-ty sight.—

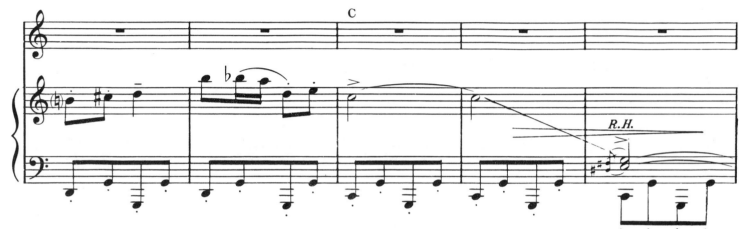

CHILDREN:

KURT:

So long, fare-well, Auf wie-der-sehn, a-dieu,— a-

dieu, A-dieu, to yieu and yieu and yieu.—

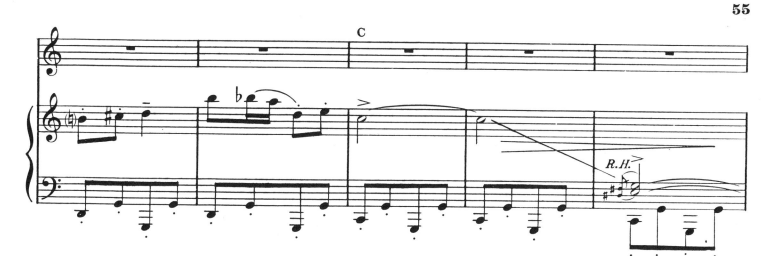

CHILDREN:

So long, fare - well, Au' - voir, Auf wie - der - sehn, _ I'd

like to stay and taste my first cham - pagne. _

56

CHILDREN: FRIEDRICH:

So long, fare-well, Auf wie-der-sehn, good - bye,_ I

leave and heave a sigh and say good - bye,_ good - bye._

Meno mosso
BRIGITTA:

I'm

LOUISA:

glad to go, I can-not tell a lie._ I flit, I float, I

1237-6

57

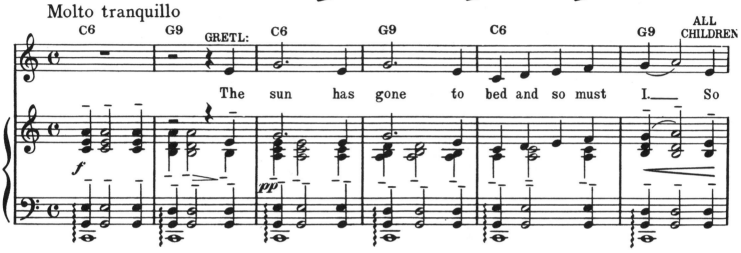

Molto tranquillo

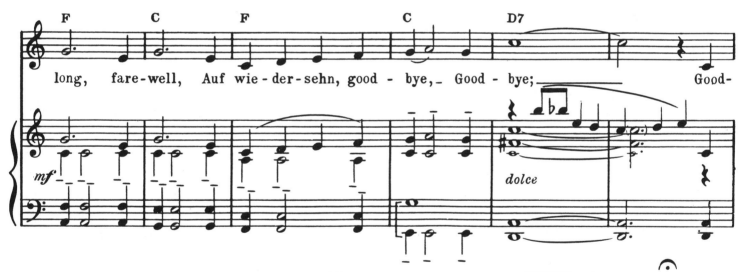

1237-6

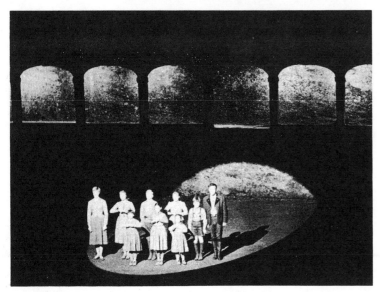

Photos courtesy 20th Century-Fox Film Corporation

Photo by Toni Frissell

Photo by Friedman-Abeles

Climb Ev'ry Mountain

Words by
OSCAR HAMMERSTEIN II

Music by
RICHARD RODGERS

Maestoso

Piano

ff

Refrain *(with deep feeling, like a prayer)*

Climb ev - 'ry moun - tain, search high and low,

mf

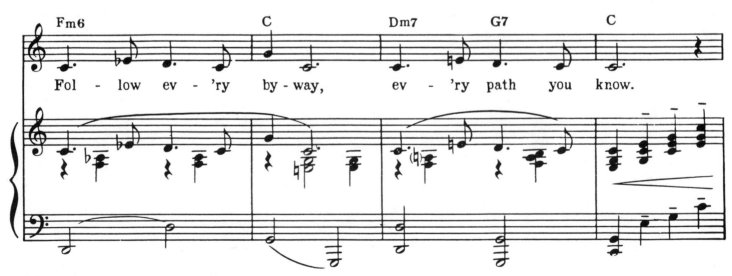

Fol - low ev - 'ry by - way, ev - 'ry path you know.

1079-3

Copyright © 1959 by Richard Rodgers and Oscar Hammerstein II
Copyright Renewed
WILLIAMSON MUSIC owner of publication and allied rights throughout the world.
International Copyright Secured   All Rights Reserved

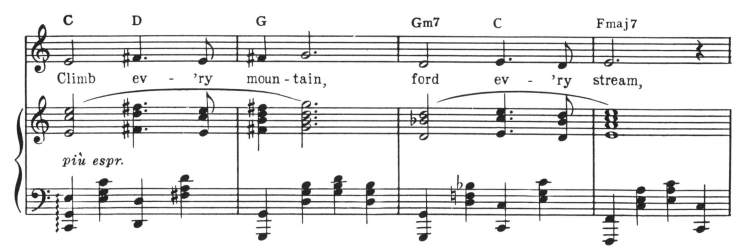

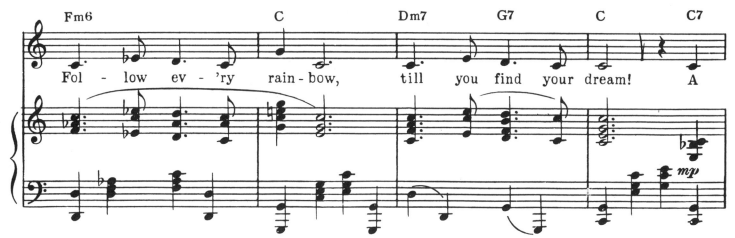

62

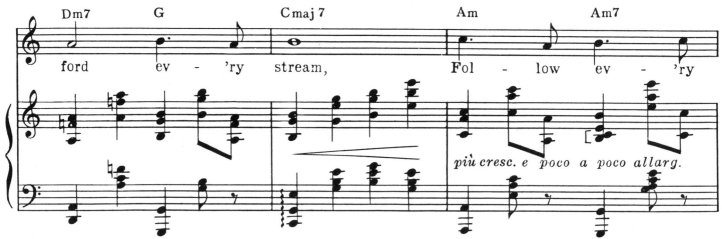

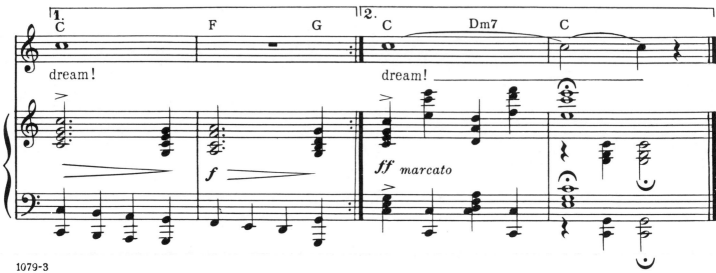

An Ordinary Couple

Words by
OSCAR HAMMERSTEIN II

Music by
RICHARD RODGERS

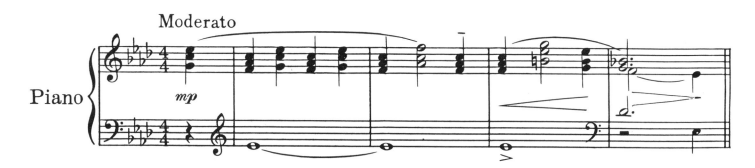

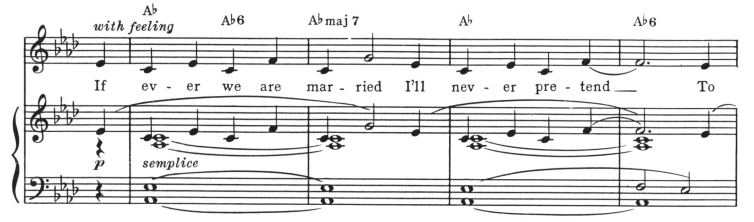

If ev-er we are mar-ried I'll nev-er pre-tend___ To

an-y dream of an-y great-er glo-ry_____ Than just to be your

hus-band, your lov-er, your friend,— And live with you an old and sim-ple

Copyright © 1959 by Richard Rodgers and Oscar Hammerstein II
Copyright Renewed
WILLIAMSON MUSIC owner of publication and allied rights throughout the world.
International Copyright Secured   All Rights Reserved

Refrain (*with very warm expression*)

An or - din - ar - y coup - le is all we'll ev - er be, For all I want of liv - ing is to

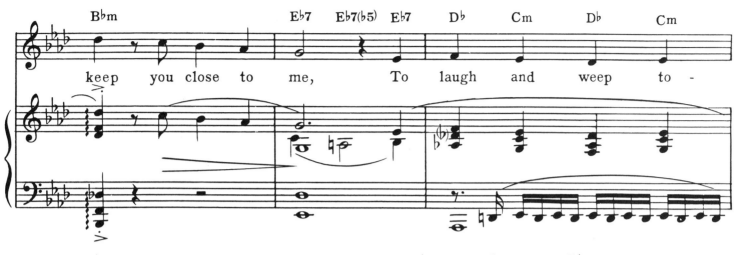

keep you close to me, To laugh and weep to -

geth - er, While time goes on its

flight, To kiss you ev - 'ry

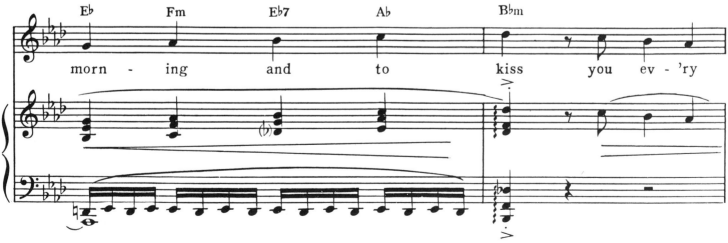

morn - ing and to kiss you ev - 'ry

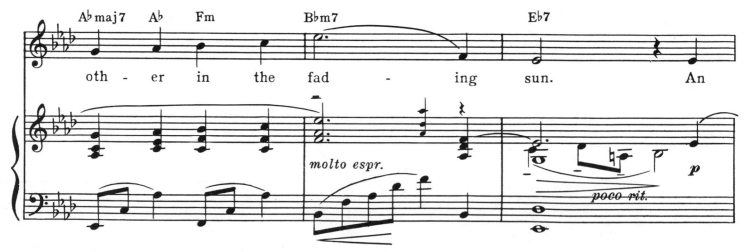

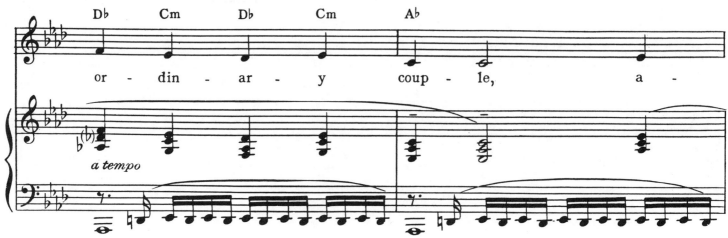

1078-5

1078-5

DRAWBAR ORGANS
Upper: 54 8754 323
Lower: (00) 6654 302(0)
Pedal: 53 (4-Fast Decay)
Vib: set V-2, Off
Percussion: Off

ALL OTHER ORGANS
Upper: Diapason & Cello 16'
      Trumpet, Flute & String 8'
      Flute & String 4'
Lower: Diapason, Flute & Viole 8'
      Flute & String 4'
Pedal: 16' & 8' suitable
Vib./Trem: Off (light or medium
            prepared for)

WEDDING PROCESSIONAL
from "THE SOUND OF MUSIC"
Arranged by Ashley Miller

Lyrics by OSCAR HAMMERSTEIN II
(Lyrics not included)

Music by RICHARD RODGERS

Tempo di marcia, maestoso

Manuals

Pedal

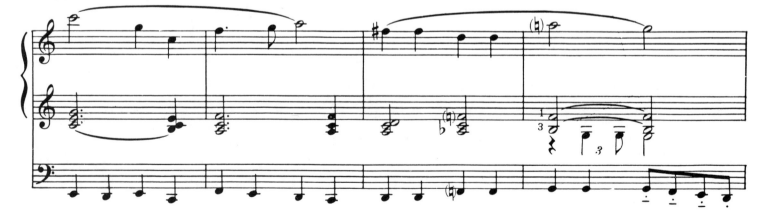

WEDDING PROCESSIONAL

Copyright © 1959 by Richard Rodgers and Oscar Hammerstein II
Copyright Renewed
WILLIAMSON MUSIC owner of publication and allied rights throughout the world.
International Copyright Secured   All Rights Reserved

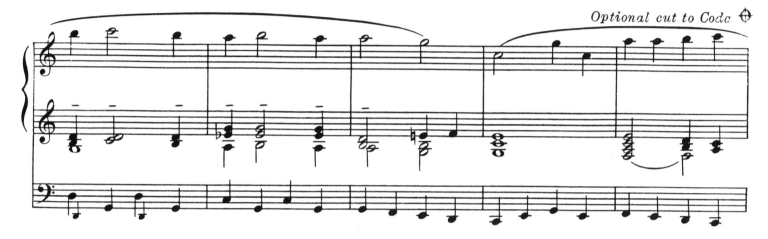

Optional cut to Coda ⊕

D.S. al Coda

𝄋

Optional Variation

Upper 50 8004 323

Off 8′ stops; add 2′

Lower (00) 6884 302
add 8′ Tuba or other 8′ solo

opt. rit.

1239-4

⊕ Coda

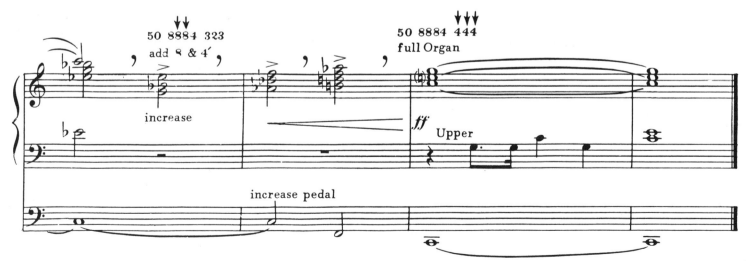

50 8884 323
add 8 & 4′
increase

50 8884 444
full Organ
ff Upper

increase pedal

Photos courtesy 20th Century-Fox Film Corporation

"The Sound Of Music"

Edelweiss

(Pronounce: Ā-dl-vise)

Words by
OSCAR HAMMERSTEIN II

Music by
RICHARD RODGERS

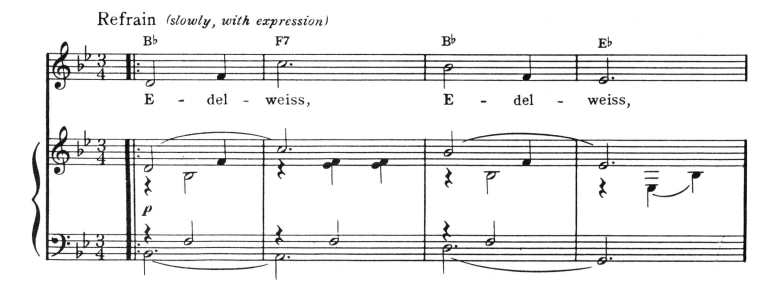

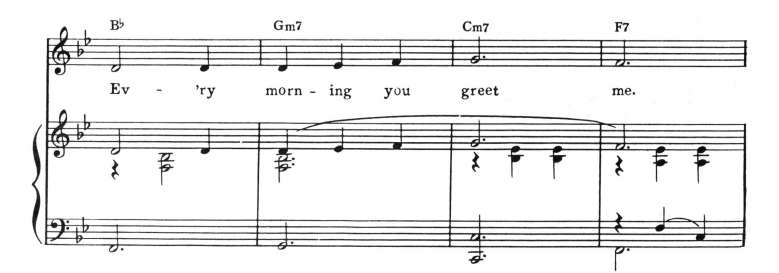

1080-3

Copyright © 1959 by Richard Rodgers and Oscar Hammerstein II
Copyright Renewed
WILLIAMSON MUSIC owner of publication and allied rights throughout the world.
International Copyright Secured   All Rights Reserved

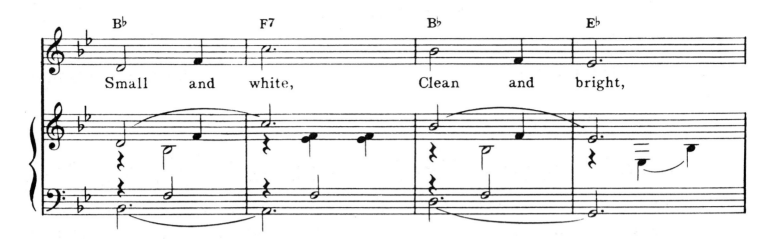

Small and white, Clean and bright,

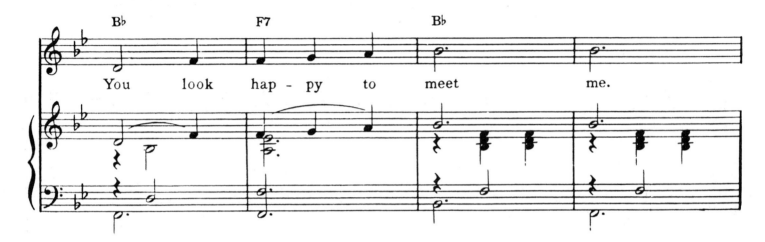

You look hap - py to meet me.

Blos - som of snow, may you bloom and grow,

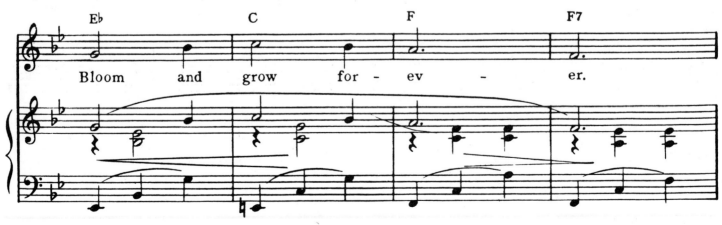

Bloom and grow for - ev - er.

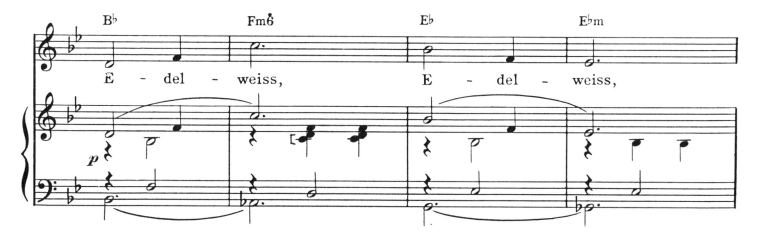

Ē - del - weiss, E - del - weiss,

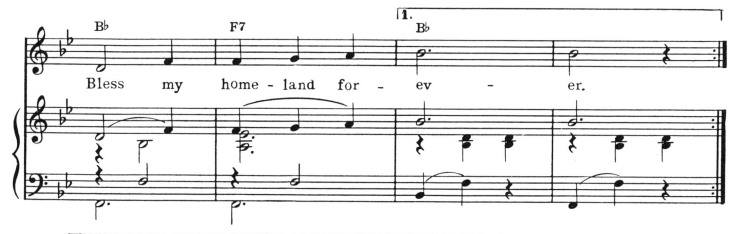

Bless my home - land for - ev - er.

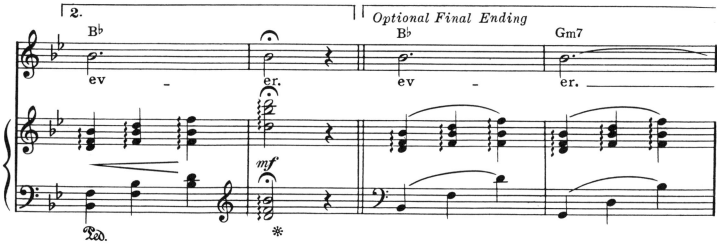

ev - er. ev - er.